Mint Tea from a Copper Pot

Mint Tea from a Copper Pot
and other tanka tales
by
Amelia Fielden

Acknowledgements

Many thanks to Marilyn Humbert, leader of the Bottlebrush Tanka Group, for her editorial eye and careful proofreading of the original manuscript.

Mint Tea from a Copper Pot and other tanka tales
ISBN 978 1 74027 804 1
Copyright © text Amelia Fielden 2013
Cover photograph (taken by David Harris) shows Amelia with Haylie and Stephen Bleakley-Harris at Pearl Beach on the NSW Central Coast, 1 October 2011
Cover design by 'pling, Canberra

First published 2013
Reprinted 2023

GINNINDERRA PRESS
PO Box 3461 Port Adelaide 5015
www.ginninderrapress.com.au

Contents

Preface	9
Prologue: Born in Australia	11
First Magpie	12
In the Twelfth Month	13
Sydney Sundays	15
Night Games	17
Across the Ocean	19
My First and Only Miai	20
Of Love, Marriage & Kanji: A True Story	26
'And is there honey still for tea?'	29
Mint Tea from a Copper Pot	30
On the Island of Malta	32
Regretting Nothing	33
'Aye, there's the rub'	35
Apple Cake	36
'Please, Sir, I want some more'	39
After the Storm, a Rainbow Lorikeet	45
A Tale of Two Cakes	46
Second Sundays in Fifth Months	48
Through the Looking Glass	49
The New Year's Tanka Poetry Gathering at the Imperial Court in Tokyo	50
In the Autumn of My Life	54
The Love Affair Continues: Japan, May 2010	55
Daisy Chains	58
Yellow Balloons	59
Time Passes	60
Just Sitting There	62
The Longest Week	63
'now that April's there'	65

Ups and Downs	67
Black Butterfly	68
Discovering Gabriola Island, British Columbia, July 2011	69
Not a Love Song, But…	71
Stars in My Eyes	72
Brief Idyll in Busselton, April 2012	73
21 April 2012	77
May 2012: Another Autumn in Canberra	78
On the Edge	79
The Piano Lesson, 13 August 2012	81
And So To Asilomar	82
Wisteria	88
My Golden Boy	89
The Element of Water	90
Not in an Aviary	94
Hydrangeas – for Elinor	99
Home for Christmas 2012: Back to the Beginning	100
Afterword: 'I'll be seeing you in all the old familiar places'	102
Acknowledgements	104
About the Author	106

the passage
*   from horizon to shore*
*   of a speedboat*
*   no swifter than the passing*
of my seventy years

This book is dedicated with devotion to
Haylie and Stephen in the hope that in
reading these tales they will come to
know more about their Grandma
Amelia's life.

> *'love, oh love,*
> *careless love'* – they've gone again*
> *and I am left*
> *sweeping the leaves fallen*
> *from this butterfly tree*

* from the song 'Careless Love' of obscure origins, which became a traditional jazz blues standard from the early twentieth century on

Preface

What are tanka tales?

Quite simply they are stories told in tanka poetry interspersed with flexible amounts of prose.

utamonogatari (poem stories), the general descriptor in Japan for this hybrid genre, were being written and enjoyed there from almost 1,200 years ago. The earliest extant Japanese tanka tales form the ninth-century book in 125 chapters called the *Ise Monogatari*, or *Tales of Ise* (Ise being a place name), which is basically a collection of poems each preceded by a very brief prose story. Many such books followed the *Ise Monogatari* in Japan, where tanka tales are extensive and well-established in the classical literary canon. Contemporary Japanese prose plus tanka writing is more likely to be in the form of poetic diaries, or often essays – on places at home and overseas – illustrated by poetry, rather than fictional stories.

In recent times, pieces of creative writing of greatly varying lengths, content and style, which combine prose and tanka, have been appearing in English language poetry journals and anthologies usually under the designation of 'tanka prose'. Based on the Japanese *utamonogatari*, 'tanka tales' seems to me the best umbrella term to cover this very wide range of writings one can see now, from autobiographical fragments and diary entries, to descriptions of natural scenes, journeys and foreign locales, and (apparently fictional) stories.

Here I am presenting desultory tanka tales, and some tanka strings without prose, from my own life, in a kind of rough chronological order.

I do hope you will enjoy exploring them!

Amelia Fielden

Prologue: Born in Australia

in the beginning
the smell of the ocean
Sydney's blue skies
my grandmother singing
Irish lullabies

autumn winds blow
over this southern land –
friends write to me
of Japanese blossoms
opening with spring warmth

three black dogs
frolicking on a white lawn
in a city
where snow seldom falls –
this I want to remember

a posse
of kookaburras
stalking the dawn
with bursts of laughter –
too serious, my life

broader, taller
that eucalypt has flourished
through all the years
I've been elsewhere seeking
my 'blue bird of happiness'

First Magpie

Family facts locate this memory somewhere in my third year of life.

Harnessed into a wooden high chair, I am sitting alone in a sunny kitchen.

On the high chair tray is a half-eaten banana, and my white stuffed dog, Pongo.

Soft music is coming from the radio.

> *all senses*
> *satisfied for now*
> *alone*
> *not lonely…on the sill*
> *a magpie chortles*

In the Twelfth Month

I have always loved December. The first month of summer on the Australian calendar, it is already hot and sunny.

There were grey times, though, in the December of 1941 – when I was born, soon after Pearl Harbour was bombed – and in the following summers of World War II.

> *on that headland*
> *of my infancy,*
> *guns mounted*
> *against the expected*
> *Japanese invasion*

With my country still at war, and before I was old enough to understand the Christian Christmas story, I became a victim of the great polio epidemic, losing two Decembers from my life.

> *Christmas Eve*
> *a boy child lying*
> *in the next bed*
> *cried himself to death –*
> *Santa came next morning*

A dark start to my life, but for the last sixty-three years December has endowed me with a wealth of love and companionship from family and friends – plus the bliss of swimming in the summer waves of the Pacific Ocean under an azure sky.

> *in my youth*
> *always the singing sea*
> *in senior years*
> *still pleasure in the surge*
> *below the lighthouse*

And now I am a grandmother, the rich days of December continue.

> *my grandchildren*
> *call me from America*
> *on Skype, perform*
> *a piano duet –*
> *more Christmas miracles*

Sydney Sundays

in Hyde Park
the great fountain sprays
on and on
through decades of change
unchanging memories

Although I've lived many years in many places since then, those Sydney Sundays with my father, when I was a child of six, seven, eight, nine, remain vivid mental souvenirs of innocent enjoyment and discovery.

off to town
in a 'toast rack' tram
with Daddy,
my patent leather shoes
not touching the floor

We get off the tram opposite David Jones, a multistoreyed treasure trove, but of course it's closed on Sundays.

Then we take the short path across Hyde Park, pausing a while to watch sparrows bathing and fluttering in the fountain. A huge, wonderful fountain with mythical figures and bronze turtles and water spouting all around.

Crossing a busy road, we pop into St Mary's cathedral, say a quick prayer excusing our absence from regular mass and asking for our loved ones – including Biddy, the cocker spaniel – to be kept safe. Daddy tells me again how before I was born he joined the crowd of onlookers inside here for the wedding of a touring Italian opera star, Amelita Galli-Curci. And how she sang the Ave Maria in front of the altar, so beautiful.

Next – and I'm always allowed the choice – it's the museum or the art gallery. If it happens to be raining, I choose the nearby museum, dawdle by the dioramas and linger over the gemstones on the top floor.

On fine Sundays – and they are mostly fine – I take the double treat of sitting on the grass in the Domain, watching the antics of the competing speakers, while we eat our cheese and Vegemite sandwiches, and then go into the gallery.

> *no microphones*
> *permitted, a speaker*
> *outperformed*
> *by kookaburras*
> *high in the Moreton Bay fig*

Those afternoons in the lofty rooms of the gallery… Daddy always asks which pictures appeal to me most and why. We stand in front of my favourites for as long as I like, talking about their stories, the way they are painted, the colours. He reminds me that his cousin Harry is an artist, that's his job. We have a print of Uncle Harry's prize-winning self-portrait on the sideboard at home.

In summer, our day out is extended by ice cream cones and a stroll down through the Botanic Gardens to the harbour. Yellow and green ferries glide in and out of the quay. There's a terminus here, where we can catch the train back to Coogee and the cream house with a pomegranate tree in its front garden.

> *though twin spires*
> *still pierce the Sydney blue*
> *here on earth*
> *no father now to lead*
> *the way into St Mary's*

Night Games

When I was a teenager in Australia…long, long ago…tennis parties under floodlights were all the vogue.

> *Sydney's sultry dark*
> *pushed back into the sky*
> *by columns*
> *of artificial light,*
> *the thud of tennis balls*

When I was a teenager, white was de rigeur for tennis: boys wore white shirts and shorts, girls, tiny white dresses, both sexes white socks and sand shoes.

That night I dared to be different; not for the first, nor the last, time in my life.

> *from under*
> *my brief white tennis frock*
> *I flashed*
> *legs clad in scarlet tights…*
> *just to see what might happen*

He happened. My first lover.

In a 'mixed doubles' draw, I faced a tall, dark, handsome young man, who introduced himself as the older brother of my cousin's classmate.

Neither of us remembers whom we partnered or which pair won the match.

But we both remember him walking me home the long way round. And those first kisses as the surf pounded the shore below the sandhills of Coogee…

Since that night, we've accumulated between us fifty-five years of lives, including four careers, five spouses, nine children, ten grandchildren, and a loving relationship which endures throughout it all.

> *my loyal friend*
> *first met playing tennis,*
> *his dear hands*
> *now too arthritic*
> *to wield a racquet*

Across the Ocean

How many times since childhood have I gazed on the waves of the Pacific, fantasising what lay over the horizon.

Now I've left that near horizon far, far, behind; I'm about to land in another hemisphere.

The Country Upstairs...will Japan be all I have read of in Colin Simpson's book?

Will I fall in love with its foreignness, as once I fell in love with the hometown boy who wrote his fond inscription on a blank page of that book, 'so that you can tear it out if you want to forget me'.

> *choosing*
> *this distance*
> *choosing*
> *to change – and yet*
> *so much to remember*

My First and Only *Miai*

It was back in the olden days, May 1963. An Australian who had never been overseas, I'd arrived a week and a half earlier at Haneda airport, on a flight from Sydney that touched down first in Manila and then in Hong Kong.

My supervisor-to-be, Professor Hiroji Matsumura, and one of his female honours students from Nagoya University, Naoko (acting as his chaperone!), were at the airport to meet me. A taxi took us from Haneda on a slow, stop-start, ride through the midnight streets of Tokyo, which, though quiet and almost deserted, had traffic lights in operation every block or so.

Eventually we were deposited at the old Imperial Hotel in Hibiya, there to sleep the remainder of the night. Our rooms were in the long since demolished and 'reformed' low-rise, be-columned, building designed by Frank Lloyd Wright, which was one of a few iconic structures left standing after the World War II bombings of Tokyo.

Two days' sightseeing in the capital, then we journeyed to Nagoya on the Tōkaidō line, in a comfortable 'express' train which took almost five hours.

During those initial two days in Japan, many things had amazed me – such as a subway train sliding into the third floor of a Shibuya department store, little drawstring plastic bags filled with water and goldfish, hung from the hat-stand of a coffee shop in Yotsuya, the iris streams at Meiji Shrine, the giant straw sandal at the Sensōji temple in Asakusa.

But I was truly astonished, on my first Friday afternoon at the university, when Professor Matsumura dismissed me from his study, bidding me to be ready in my 'best dress' (my interpretation of his vague wording), at three o'clock the following day – at which time, precisely, he would collect me from the Asian students' hostel where I had been staying and take me to my *miai*.

Now, as a serious student of Japanese language and society, I was well aware of the meaning of *miai*, the 'seeing meeting' which was the first stage in the modern version of a Japanese arranged marriage. I had read that, through a *nakōdo*, a 'go-between', parents exchanged extensive dossiers on sons and daughters deemed ripe for marriage. If and when agreement was reached within the families that the principals concerned were willing to 'have a look at each other', a meeting was arranged. This meeting – normally held on neutral territory such as the lobby of a Western-style hotel, or in a high-class restaurant, was orchestrated by the go-between (customarily a friend, neighbour or relative of one of the parties) and attended also by the four parents and the two young people. The prospective bride and groom, flanked by parents, exchanged a few formal remarks and then kept their heads down, while the elders discussed whatever was deemed appropriate. Later, both sides would report back – usually by telephone – to the go-between, as to whether they wished to proceed with a further meeting. And so on…

That day when Professor Matsumura summarily announced my *miai*, I was twenty-one years old, then considered a suitable age for a bride. However, I hadn't come to Japan to be married, but to spend a year researching classical Japanese literature, specifically the tenth-century *Eiga Monogatari* (on which Professor Matsumura was the greatest living expert), under the auspices of the grandly titled Saionji Memorial Scholarship.

To my anxious probing, the professor responded that my *miai* was not for the purposes of introducing a possible marriage partner, but to determine where I was to live for the next twelve months. *Aa sō…*

My request from Australia had been for a 'homestay' with a Japanese family, as I was eager for a total immersion experience. To my disappointment, on arrival in Nagoya I was placed in a hostel, the sole female amongst male students from other parts of Asia. The professor had muttered words to the effect that this was only temporary accommodation, and exhorted me to *gaman*. In the event, the lock on my bedroom door in the hostel proved more useful than a *gaman* ('putting up with it') attitude. Anyway, hopefully this was it: the end of hostel dwelling, and a decision on a homestay venue. *Banzai* ('hurrah')!

On the day of my first and only *miai*, Professor Matsumura and his wife – who rarely appeared in public – escorted me by taxi to the small, wooden home in Nagoya suburb of our *makōdo*, Mrs Nishi. I never did discover Mrs Nishi's relationship to any of those concerned, but she fulfilled her role with rhythmic gravity.

We were ushered by Mrs Nishi into an immaculate six-mat tatami room. Around a large, low table were already kneeling two couples, splendidly garbed in formal kimono: Mrs Hisazaki with her daughter Nariko, and Mrs Tashiro with her daughter Reiko. Introductions were made, greeting exchanged.

Then, amid almost total silence, the eight of us present were served porcelain cups of 'red' (that is, Ceylon) tea with lemon slices, and large pieces of a strawberry and cream sponge cake, on matching Noritake plates with little gold forks, by a young maid in a plain workaday kimono. Feeling overawed by the atmosphere of restraint, I did not venture to start a conversation, but as noiselessly as possible consumed my tea and cake. When I looked up from my empty plate, I saw to my embarrassment that all seven other pieces of cake were still on their plates, albeit with various (small) portions removed. We sat there for a further thirty minutes – yes, I could manage *seiza* in those days without losing sensation in my legs – while a few remarks were exchanges. Those remarks were so brief and inconsequential that I couldn't remember, even immediately afterwards, just what had been said.

On a signal from the professor, his wife and I rose. To the accompaniment of much deep bowing, and expression of appreciation to our hostess, we left the house and entered our waiting taxi. The taxi driver had been patient, and so, I considered, had I; but now I couldn't hold back from asking, 'Well, what was decided?'

Gazing at me with gentle reproof in his eyes ('will this foreign girl ever understand our ways'), Professor Matsumura replied, 'You are to spend half of your year with the Tashiro family, and half with the Hisazaki family, of course.' Of course! *Aa, sō desu ka...*

And so it came to pass: the very next day I went to live with the Tashiros, near Nanzan University, for six months; and just before the New Year of 1964, I transferred to the Hisazaki family of doctors, who ran a private hospital near Higashiyama.

In due course, I discovered that the young ladies at the *miai* were students of Professor Matsumura at the Joshi Tandai (Women's Short Course University) where he taught in addition to his primary post at Meidai (Nagoya University). On my request for a homestay, the professor had advertised me at those two institutions. The only takers for the *gaijin** homestay assignment – which I learned later was considered an extremely courageous undertaking – were the Tashiro and the Hisazaki families. It must be remembered that was almost half a century ago, when there were none of the now prolific student exchange programs; and Nagoya was not yet an international city.

In both cases the parents' initial motivation in offering me a home was to add 'English conversation', to the *hanayome keiko* ('bride lessons') of tea ceremony, flower-arranging and piano playing with which Reiko Tashiro and Nariko Hisazaki were already occupied, in addition to their Japanese literature studies at the Joshi Tandai.

* 'gaijin' is the Japanese word for 'foreigner'; it has a slightly derogatory connotation.

An only child in my birth family, I thus acquired two delightful Japanese sisters; they were born in the same year as I, but several months earlier, making them, as each reminded me from time to time, my *o-ne san* ('she who must be obeyed elder sister'.)

Reiko and Nariko were wonderful sisters and companions to me in the first of my many years in Japan. They were not, however, as motivated as my two perpetually kimono clad 'mothers' towards the English conversation thing. Once they had ascertained my degree of proficiency in Japanese, Reiko and Nariko seemed to prefer engaging with me and having fun in their native tongue, rather than trying to learn English.

One of the first things I asked of Reiko, when I had settled into her family home with her mother, father (owner of a small export business), older brother, younger sister, younger brother, maid, two cats and a watchdog, was a solution to the 'strawberry sponge cake mystery '– why everyone but me had left most of that delicious confection uneaten.

Vive la difference culturelle! Reiko explained that, by Japanese custom, the hostess was bound to provide food and drink; and the guests (hungry or not) were bound to sample both – but not, like in Australia, to clean their plates as an indication of appreciation. Rather, it was considered inelegant to devour a whole piece of cake (uh oh).

Of course I continued to make strawberry sponge cake type gaffes throughout my time in Nagoya. But under the kindly guidance of the professor, and my two big-hearted Japanese families, we all survived my homestay experience and I learned a lot.

As to the future: Reiko and Nariko, still single, after multiple genuine *miai*, and wearing the beautiful *furisode* ('hanging sleeves') kimono befitting their status, were bridesmaids when I married a young British diplomat. This wedding took place at Christ Church on the Bluff of Yokohama, one week after the end of the Tokyo Olympics, to which I had been seconded as interpreter for the Trinidad/Tobago team.

On her way to catch the new *shinkansen* 'bullet train' home to Nagoya after my wedding, Nariko met (in rather unusual circumstances) the young medical intern whom she was to marry the following year – but that's another story.

Much, much later, after I had divorced him, Reiko married the British diplomat and, to my infinite regret, dropped out of my life – yet another story.

> *here she stands*
> *in the old album*
> *our best friend,*
> *his next wife, between him*
> *and my pregnant belly*

Forty-nine years after my first and only *miai*, Nariko, however, is still one of my closest friends in the world. We see each other either in Japan or Australia most years; and my second husband and I, having stood *in loco parentis* at the Sydney wedding of her elder son, are now honorary godparents to her two grandsons.

Time passes, but the memories stand still.

> *ah, my friend*
> *once more we are meeting*
> *soon to part…*
> *almost half a century*
> *and still this pattern holds*

Of Love, Marriage & *Kanji*: A True Story

There once lived in far off Nagoya a lovely young lady called Nariko. Born in May 1941, she was the seventh child and fifth daughter of a prosperous medical family.

For reasons best known to himself, Nariko's father entered her on the family register with the same *kanji* for her given name as her immediately elder sister. Dr Hisazaki specified that, while the older girl was know as Seiko – '*sei*' being the *on yomi* ('Chinese reading') of the *kanji* – her sister would be called Nariko, '*nari*' being its *kun yomi* ('Japanese reading').

Seiko and Nariko were close in age and became the best of friends. They sometimes amused themselves confusing people with their identical written names.

While Nariko was still completing her education at a tertiary college, Seiko had a *miai* at which she was introduced to a suitable young man with a view to matrimony. In due course, the couple wed, then moved to New York when the young man's company posted him there.

When Seiko was due to deliver her first child, Nariko was dispatched to America to help the new family.

Some months later, on her return to Nagoya, Nariko received a curious phone call.

'May I speak with Miss Seiko, please?'

'I'm sorry, Seiko is not here right now.'

'When do you expect her back?'

'Well, she's still in New York. They won't be returning to Japan with the baby until the end of her husband's posting.'

'Huh? My apologies; I must have the wrong number...'

'Just a moment. Perhaps you want me – I'm Seiko's younger sister, Nariko.'

The continuing conversation established that young Dr Yōji Nakamura had been given, by a mutual friend who fancied herself as a matchmaker, a note with Nariko's name – in *kanji* only – and phone number on it. Explaining something of their circumstances to each other, they then agreed to exchange photos and talk again in the near future.

At the time, Yōji was living in Tokyo, working all hours of day and night at his university's hospital. Nariko was a student in Nagoya and also much relied upon by her mother to assist with the running of a large and complex household. It appeared difficult for them to meet. Moreover, Nariko was averse to a formal *miai*, having witnessed all her older siblings going through that process.

However, the would-be go-between did not give up easily. She discovered that Nariko was to attend a wedding in Yokohama on a certain Saturday in October, returning home by the new *shinkansen* 'bullet train' from Tokyo station the same evening. Unbeknown to Nariko, the go-between apprised Yōji of Nariko's schedule.

That inclement October evening, as Nariko stood on the platform waiting for her train, she was hailed by a very tall young man wearing a shabby, sodden raincoat and muddy knee-length rubber boots. Shaking drops of water from his shaggy hair, Yōji introduced himself. They had just time to make a few inconsequential remarks when the signal was given for Nariko to board.

Many years later, when I sat with them at their dining table in Tokyo, hearing how they had come together, my dear hosts added these comments:

Yōji: 'I was sharing a flat with a mate. We were so poor, we only had one umbrella and one raincoat between us. That day it was my turn for the raincoat.'

Nariko: 'He was tall and he had a nice face but he was such a mess, so very wet. We were both too shy to say much. Then, from the window of the train as it pulled out I watched him waving, and I thought to myself, "Right, that's the man I'm going to marry."'

A week later Nariko's doctor father received a phone call. Never one to mince words, he called out, 'Oy, Nariko! There's a guy on the line, name of Nakamura, says he wants to marry you. Do you want to marry him, or what?'

'Yes, Papa. I'll marry him.'

So that was that. They only saw each other three times before the wedding – including the initial brief encounter at Tokyo station. Then in 2005, Nariko and Yōji celebrated their ruby wedding anniversary in the company of two sons, two grandsons and the foreign friend whose wedding had been the catalyst for their first meeting, and to whom they had related the story of their 'non-*miai*' courtship.

> *pretty in pink*
> *a smiling grandmother*
> *treasured still*
> *this patient companion*
> *of my young gaijin years*

'And is there honey still for tea?'*
Oxford, Early Summer 1970

A short, final holiday in England before our two-year posting in Morocco.

My memories of that time in Oxford, more than forty years ago, are distilled into the clear recollection of a single afternoon.

What I see now in my mind's eye is more like a brief documentary film, than the usual mental snapshot.

> *cotton frocks*
> *cucumber sandwiches*
> *orange pekoe*
> *from a china teapot…*
> *and a resident robin*

Behind Aunt Anne's house on the Woodstock Road meandered a deep garden.

A quintessentially English garden: green green lawn, bright flower beds bordered with pansies, a white gazebo – and to my little daughter's delight, a small goldfish pond.

One afternoon Aunt Anne decreed our teatime should be a picnic in the garden.

Just the three of us. And a resident robin who flew into the peaceful apple tree whenever Maria toddled too close.

> *one of us is gone*
> *one was too young then*
> *to recall scenes*
> *that will only live*
> *for as long as I do*

* This is the final line of the long, elegiac poem 'The Old Vicarage, Grantchester', written in 1912 by the English poet Rupert Brooke.

Mint Tea from a Copper Pot

> *Morocco:*
> *gold-spiced memories*
> *of your birth*
> *by the river Bouregreg*
> *eucalypts shading your sleep*

A peaceful suburb of Rabat one hot Sunday afternoon in early July, 1971. You are only ten days old, my precious daughter, Miriam.

'The king is dead. Long live the revolution!' from the radio a voice bellowing in Arabic and French, over and over.

Alerted to an attack on the royal birthday celebrations by his Japanese colleague, 'Monsieur' has rushed to the embassy in town to make cable contact with the Foreign Office in London.

I cancel Fatima's weekly outing. She locks our high wrought-iron gates, bolts our cedar doors.

Then we feed the children, drink mint tea and wait. And drink mint tea and wait. And wait.

The king is not dead. As peasant soldiers under the orders of dis-affected army officers burst into the coastal compound, sniping at panicked guests and golf caddies, Hassan II has secreted himself in a turret bathroom of his summer palace.

He is to survive this and half a dozen further coups and assassination attempts, and will die of heart disease at the age of seventy many years on.

The revolution is short-lived. Rebels take over the treasury – but not the post office – and there are several days of skirmishes through the centre of Rabat. Eventually royal Moroccan troops loyal to their despotic ruler prevail.

The French-educated leaders of the coup are executed, swiftly, publicly. Nothing more is heard of the soldiers they commanded.

The merry-go-round of diplomatic functions starts up again.

But this is no longer my paradise on earth.

> *spilling over*
> *tall whitewashed walls*
> *scarlet*
> *bouganvillea*
> *screams and gunshots*

On the Island of Malta

I lived the first three years of my thirties
One daughter started school
The other learned to walk and talk
      We spent many blissful hours in the sapphire sea.

A wonderful man and I fell in love; both devoted
to our families, we did not act on our feelings.

My mother came to visit and was injured in a car accident.

More than fifty pavlovas for dinner parties were
baked in our bottled-gas oven.

An unexpected pregnancy brought first joy, then sorrow when
it failed.

      The past does not die

      my almost son
      would be thirty-nine
      this year
      every year, I light
      his candles from the stars

Regretting Nothing*

> *all my life*
> *smelling the sweetpeas*
> *mauve, pink, white*
> *in a pair of crystal vases*
> *on my mother's dressing table*

Evening in Paris, the intense perfume released from its small blue glass flask like an invisible genie, whenever Mummy was dressing for a ball.

Always that perfume, always a corsage of fresh flowers.

Dabbing a little Evening in Paris as a special treat behind my infant ears, she would kiss me goodnight and, with a swirl of silky skirts, be gone.

> *I remember*
> *no fragrance from the orchids*
> *my mother wore,*
> *only their vibrant colours*
> *pinned on her evening gowns*

Evening in Paris, at the end of wonderful hours walking with our baby daughter in her pushchair, around the spring city: the Left Bank, Notre Dame, and back to the Place de L'Opera. Finding a bar which sold hard-boiled eggs, for a simple supper.

> *so young*
> *so open to experience*
> *Japan, England,*
> *Morocco, France, Malta*
> *ours for the tasting*

---

* Edith Piaf sang so strongly, 'non, je ne regrette rien'.

Evening in Paris. Not so young any more. Not so old either. Perhaps half of my life behind me now. Rediscovering this 'city of light' in winter's darkness, I'm in love again.

> *new French-blue blouse –*
> *under a snow sky*
> *in Paris*
> *the last time I risked*
> *everything for love*

> *icicles hung*
> *from the Eiffel Tower*
> *at dusk*
> *I'm lusting for the heat*
> *of his hotel room*

> *'the past*
> *is another country',*
> *and I wear*
> *Worth's Je Reviens,*
> *hopefully…*

Midnight in Paris. An actor is transported back in time when he pauses beside the Seine as a clock strikes twelve. I am flooded with recollections of my own lost eras.

> *casting his net*
> *with those first haunting bars*
> *the clarinettist*
> *hauls me up to the stars:*
> *Midnight in Paris*

'Aye, there's the rub'*

This January afternoon of 2003 is hot and very dry, but the climate in the Tradies' Club as we dance to the cheerful Black Mountain Jazz Band is air-conditioned chill.

Suddenly, a strident interruption: the broadcast message urges all those who live in certain areas of the capital to leave immediately and return to their homes to defend them against an out-of-control bushfire.

It couldn't be happening here…could it?

Outside, the sky is a doomsday purplish black – at only three o'clock. A dense quilt of smoke smothers our suburb for many hours while leaves are cleared from roof gutters, cars packed ready for evacuation.

By morning the peril has passed, and we are still here.

Then, from the radio we learn more and more of the devastation and tragedies one day has brought to Canberra.

> *an Olympian*
> *loses his medals, and his dog –*
> *those who've survived,*
> *how do they sleep? 'to sleep*
> *perchance to dream…'*

---

* Hamlet's famous long soliloquy in the Shakespeare play of the same name includes this line: 'To sleep, perchance to Dream; Aye, there's the rub.'

Apple Cake

Twenty years and more after my mother died, I began making regular visits to 'Aunty' Bette, not a blood relative but Mum's best friend from her teenage years onwards.

Although we had never actually lost contact – there were always cards exchanged at birthdays and Christmases – geography and the demands of her severely demented and antisocial husband had kept us apart for a long time. Then 'Uncle' Mick was gone, and I retired from the Public Service in Canberra, moving with my husband and our young labradoodles to Aunty Bette's city.

By then the dear lady was a housebound invalid, living alone with assistance from various services. Once a week or so we'd drive the short distance to her house to have coffee and cake and keep Aunty Bette company for a few hours in the morning.

> *aged aunt*
> *creaking, opens the door*
> *of her freezer*
> *to display the latest line*
> *in designer cakes*

When I say 'we', Kin and Konni, the labradoodles, were always included in these visits. Aunty Bette, a dog-lover from way back, doted on them. She was of the 'a little of what you fancy does you good', school, and slipped the furry ones many an illicit chunk of apple cake – the favourite snack of all three.

Our mornings together were mutually pleasurable, I believe. Certainly Aunty Bette showed every sign of appreciating our company, my husband always enjoys sharing with others the fun of Kin and Konni – and eating cake – and, as for me: how comfortable I felt being with the one person left on this earth who had held me the day I was born and had known me, known me intimately, throughout my childhood. And who could tell stories of the long ago days before I was even 'a twinkle in your father's eyes', when four young people played and courted in a beachside suburb of Sydney.

Time seemed to stand still those mornings. Then the 'doodles would get restless, as little ones do when the talking goes on too long, and we'd get up to go, confident there would be a next visit.

> *'bye, children'*
> *says Aunty Bette*
> *to Kin and Konni*
> *understanding fully*
> *their status in our lives*

There were many next visits to the small house in New Lambton. But finally came the day when Aunty Bette lost the use of her legs. She was hospitalised for a while, and then, sadly, there was nothing for it but a nursing home.

Both institutions looked kindly on Kin and Konni, and allowed us to take them in to be with Aunty Bette as unofficial 'therapy dogs' for a short while, much to her delight and that of the other patients around.

It wasn't very long, however, before Aunty Bette's daughter managed to have her mother moved to a nursing home in the country town where she lived, several hours' drive away. It was obviously the best thing for them both: they could be really close every day for the days that were left.

We missed our 'Aunty', though, and telephone calls came down to just a short exchange of voices:

> *tired so tired*
> *'I've lived too long' her voice*
> *whispering*
> *down a public line*
> *from the nursing home*

Ultimately there were no more telephone calls, no more Aunty Bette. I was sad, but could take comfort in the knowledge that she no longer had to put up with being old and ill and terminally weary.

What brought tears to my eyes each time, was the puzzlement of the 'doodles. Our route into the city often took us through New Lambton. Whenever the car neared the turning to Aunty Bette's street, Kin and Konni would stand up, enthusiastically wagging their tails and uttering joyful woofles.

As there were no more apple cake calls to be made, we'd drive straight on. Their tails would gradually droop, then they'd lie back in resigned silence for the rest of the trip.

'Please, Sir, I want some more'*

After retirement from full-time work as a Japanese translator, I returned to university to undertake a Master of Arts degree in Japanese Literature. The University of Newcastle, Australia, has several 'sister' relationships with tertiary institutes in Japan. One of these is with Ube Frontier University, located in the small city of Ube in Yamaguchi prefecture, Japan's 'far west'.

In September 2004 I was awarded a short-term exchange fellowship to Ube Frontier University, there to complete my Masters thesis. As my presentation for the degree was to be 'An Annotated Translation of the 2002 Tanka Collection *Hizuke no Aru Uta* (*My Tanka Diary*)', written by the high-profile contemporary poet Kawano Yūko, it seemed fitting that I should record my impressions of the period in tanka form.

Here is an abridged version of my own tanka diary for the three months from autumn into winter, when I was living in Ube. I did travel around too, mainly in Yamaguchi prefecture and in northern Kyushu; but this is just the story of Ube and me:

two days after my arrival, typhoon number 23 for 2004 hits Ube; the university is closed; my colleagues insist I stay home; nothing to do but read and watch television

>seasick waves
>lurch over breakwaters
>while umbrellas
>become ribs and rags
>in NHK's typhoon

---

* So said the boy Oliver, in Charles Dickens's novel *Oliver Twist*.

☐ *at College House, my home for the next three months*

not yet time
to close the books for sleep –
a chiming clock
sounds the empty hours
in the dining-kitchen

one quiet dove
on the TV antenna
at six o'clock:
like me, an early riser
or escaping from somewhere

☐ *typhoon 23 has blown away; I'm off exploring my suburb*

in scraped ground
beside a drainpipe
white daisies
living like bright words
from a self-help book

between houses
miniature rice paddies
turning gold
for autumn harvest –
the typhoon has passed

☐ *Bunkyō-cho, next to the Seven*

a quiet spell
in the local post office
no one using
the spectacles provided
for forgetful seniors

☐ *late afternoon at Tokiwa Park Eleven Shop*

barely afloat
after recent downpours
paddle boats
on a mirror-lake
among the trees and clouds

☐ *working, working, at university and in my College House room*

how brightly white
hangs tonight's crescent moon
above curved roofs
in the nebulous sky
of industrial Ube

schedule busy,
my days are quickly filled –
it's in dream time
I want to go back, back when
anything was possible

☐ *strolling in the city centre, following the 'sculpture train' of modern installations*

in Ube
proud city of sculpture,
black granite
shaping a giant donut
with a tiny shiny hole

golden fans
fluttering among the green
of summer,
a line of gingko trees
leans toward autumn

☐ *at Bōchō pool*

I kick away
composing in my head
tanka that
may not be so buoyant
when we leave the water

☐ *at supermarket Aruk*

a portly baker
beaming under his moustache
as he proudly
tells us he has been
to Bondi Beach – three times

☐ *a taste of my favourite fruit*

☐ *from the local train line to town*

first persimmon
of this Japanese autumn,
discarded skin
luminous as lacquer –
no, I regret nothing

elegance:
one snowy heron
posing
on the ridge between
yellowing rice fields

☐ *an intriguing name for a hotel! restaurant where I lunch…*

☐ *near Sunday's Sun family on Saturdays*

who makes love
in the Hotel Zoo
this wet night
when our bus bounces past,
screen-wipers lusty

a woman weeds,
listening in her cabbage patch
to the *enka*
I love to play loudly
when driving alone

☐ *at Ube Frontier University: the annual festival*

balloon balls
in a paddling pool,
multicoloured
like the dreams of those kids
who fish with paper scoops

smiles as bright
as their orange aprons,
the master chefs
of okonomiyaki
shouting '*irrashaimase*'*

☐ *28 November 2004*

☐ *a wedding at the Zenniku Hotel*

three last weeks
to last a lifetime,
but how long
will this lifetime last…
dry leaves lie in the dust
together?

the banquet
and its attendants
are ready –
how ready are bride and groom
for decades of meals

☐ *inside the Sōrinji; the kokoro† pond at the temple*

a harmony
of kimono clad ladies
attentive to
their tea ceremony master,
the tightness of tradition

across the water
a floating brocade cloak
of bright leaves
lined with gold black silver
by undulating carp

☐ *30 November, in a tiny café at Nishihirabara*

☐ *after the taikō concert*

no customers
so the cook is knitting
something in grey –
'fresh mackerel today'
she offers, then lights the gas

over Ube
a grubby evening sky with
fingernail moon:
unpoetic autumn
yet such contentment

* 'welcome'
† 'heart-shaped'

☐ *at the monthly tanka society*

   arranged
   in the austere classroom
   apricot roses,
   and three white camellias
   on a student's obi

☐ *the university president's garden workshop*

   this warm autumn
   the flowers are confused
   he tells me
   while my camera admires
   their indiscreet blooming

☐ *the start of the Hagi Okan route*

   who might come
   striding riding down
   this stony path
   from the misty mountains,
   from Hagi history?

☐ *in the Twenty-first Century Forest*

   samurai
   directed by Kurosawa
   lurking
   behind the pines, swords ready
   to swish into action

☐ *near Iwahana Station*

   winter gloom...
   overseas research
   soon to end
   but how bright the pink
   of sasanquas in bloom

☐ *a cluster of low, wooden, houses*

   shadows chilling
   persimmons strung out to dry
   beneath the eaves
   a promise of warm feasting
   within, come New Year

☐ *finishing this adventure*

hard to believe   sunset fire
I shan't shop any more   flares above the charcoal
at Marukyu –   mountain rims,
have to go home to unlearn as I'm driven too soon
the habits of these months   towards the airport lights

                        what a life:
                        lots of people to love
                        poems to write –
                        'please, Sir, I
                        want some more'

After the Storm, a Rainbow Lorikeet

on the concrete floor
a rainbow lorikeet
perfectly feathered
no breath in its body
this summer morning

I discover the dead bird lying on its back beside my car when I open the garage door.

It must have been there all night. The door was open even during yesterday's wild weather. Then I'd closed it with the remote control from inside our house, at bedtime.

How long had the lorikeet lain there? It certainly wasn't in the garage when I'd driven in the previous afternoon.

Gently I lift the spread of colours. So vivid, so insubstantial…

no blood, no blemish,
ah, a broken neck –
what was your story
beautiful bird,
and who cares about it?

I do.

Yes, I tell my husband, I know the world is sadly full of wars and famines and abused children.

But let me mourn this small tragedy on our peaceful patch.

A Tale of Two Cakes

Once upon a time, when I was a poor student in Tokyo, I happened to meet at the local railway station another poor student, who lived in the same humble lodgings. Strolling home together we came to a stop before the window of a glamorous patisserie.

'Oh, look,' exclaimed Mariko, 'mont-blanc…of course, it's autumn now.'

As an Australian raised on lamingtons and fruit cake, I had no idea what she was talking about. With a hungry gleam in her beautiful brown eyes, Mariko explained mont-blanc was a type of cup cake, topped with pale brown chestnut puree in the shape of a mountain, and crowned with a whole candied chestnut. Japanese food is very seasonal, and chestnuts are an autumn specialty.

We added up our yen and bought just one small mont-blanc between us. Back in Mariko's tiny tatami-mat room, we shared the cake and a pot of green tea. Delicious!

Two years later, diagnosed with tuberculosis, Mariko left the Piano Academy and went home to Kyushu to die.

> *sometimes I dream*
> *of that other life, and*
> *of Mariko*
> *forever twenty-three*
> *all these years I have lived*

Another era, another part of Japan. Not so poor now, I was dining in late spring with a charming university professor.

On the dessert menu I found '*ajisai* mont-blanc', 'hydrangea mont-blanc'. Curious, I asked for this when my companion ordered coffee. With a bow the waiter presented, on a plate decorated with real, purple, hydrangea petals, a classically formed mont-blanc cake, whose chestnut puree was coloured the same purple as the flower petals.

Of course…May is the season for celebrating hydrangea in Japan.

> *indulging me*
> *with the exotic cake*
> *I fancied,*
> *he smilingly denied*
> *my stronger desires*

> *he and I*
> *so much in common*
> *so much to say…*
> *both loving this country,*
> *alas not each other*

In the summer of the following year, enjoying an afternoon snack of perennial red bean buns in Kyoto with a poet colleague, I recounted to her my mont-blanc episodes.

'Ah,' she commented, 'through those two cakes you have truly experienced *aware*, the pitifully transient nature of life and love.'

> *my life*
> *is what it is, still*
> *contemplating*
> *Japanese tanka*
> *love, longing, and loss*

Second Sundays in Fifth Months

at death's door, Mum
paused, smiled and thanked me
for loving her –
I wonder if I will
be granted such grace

arum lilies
for her first Mother's Day
my daughter
her daughter and I
looking at them together

her son's fingers
tangling her long dark hair –
just yesterday
it seems, I brushed and braided
that hair…for school

in her place
iris messengers
deep purple
alone not alone
one more Mother's Day

Through the Looking Glass

When I visit my grandchildren in faraway USA, I'm in the habit of walking the family's border collie around the neighbourhood.

We often pass a little wooden house, pale yellow and as pretty as a storybook picture.

I fantasise about dwelling there in another lifetime.

One day, the front door of the pale yellow house opens.

Out steps a young woman with bright brown hair, wearing a crimson dress just like my favourite of half a century ago.

> *ruffling the fur*
> *of black and white Gypsy*
> *I pause*
> *a moment in this dream*
> *which is my reality*

The New Year's Tanka Poetry Gathering at the Imperial Court in Tokyo

On Wednesday 16 January 2008, I had the great privilege of attending this occasion, called in Japanese *Utakai Hajime*. Following a thousand-year-old tradition, it is now a national event of considerable cultural significance in which the heritage of tanka, as the standard form of Japanese poetry, is acknowledged.

Originally confined to tanka composed by members of the Imperial family and the Imperial household, this ceremony was expanded in 1879 to include tanka which were submitted by the general public, and judged of sufficient merit for presentation before the court and dignitaries. At that time, judging was still done internally by members of the Poetry Department of the Imperial Household Ministry.

After World War II, this Poetry Department was abolished; each year from 1947, prominent poets from the country at large have been appointed as *senja* ('selectors', or 'judges').

In 2007/2008 there were five distinguished poet senja, all male: Nagata Kazuhiro, Okano Hirohiko, Okai Takashi, Shino Hiroshi, Saegusa Takayuki. Their responsibility was to choose the tanka from amongst over 60,000 public submissions received by the Imperial Household Agency, on the set theme for 2008 of 'fire'. The selectors were also required to compose one tanka each on the same theme.

Since 1950, the writers of the winning poems have been permitted to attend the *Utakai Hajime*, to hear their tanka formally chanted. The ten 2008 winners, five females and five males, were all present on 16 January, along with the five selectors, seven reciters (all men) and 100 guests (ninety men and ten women). I had been invited as the guest of *senja* Professor Nagata Kazuhiro, the leading judge on this occasion and husband of high-profile poet Kawano Yūko, for whom I had been appointed official translator. And I found myself in very distinguished company indeed!

Last to enter the enormous chandeliered Western-style Pine Tree Hall where the ceremony was held were members of the Imperial Family: Emperor Akihito, Empress Michiko, Crown Prince Naruhito, his brother, Prince Fumihito and wife Princess Kiko, the Emperor's brother, Prince Masahito and wife Princess Hanako, the Emperor's aunt, Princess Yuriko, and his cousin, Princess Hisako.

In the Imperial presence, first were chanted, by the official reciters in a grave manner and with diction far removed from contemporary spoken Japanese, the ten winning tanka. Here I will quote just the tanka by the oldest, and the youngest, winner (in my translation):

> *up into the sky*
> *from which snow is quietly falling*
> *rush*
> *roaring fireworks*
> *for the Boat Launching Ceremony*
> by Ms Uomoto (aged 86)
>
> *it's so lonely*
> *watching fireworks*
> *by myself,*
> *says Dad, telephoning*
> *from his far-off work post*
> by Mr Tanaka (aged 14)

Throughout the ninety-minute formalities, the composer of each tanka was named by a master of ceremonies and stood for the recital of his or her piece.

Following the ten national winners, the MC introduced the 2008 *meshiudo*, the distinguished elderly woman poet, Miya Hideko (born in 1918), one of only six ladies present (myself included), who was wearing Japanese traditional kimono. *Meshiudo*, which means 'guest of the court', is a title conferred on a different poet each year and has the equivalence of poet laureate.

Her tanka was this:

> *from the pure white*
> *of ashes*
> *cloaking this sunken hearth*
> *rises a fire*
> *to warm the dawn*

After Mrs Miya's tanka were recited the five selectors' compositions in turn.

Here is the tanka by poet Nagata Kazuhiro:

> *the smell of a fire*
> *faintly drifting…*
> *buoyant*
> *in the twilight*
> *fly snow insects*

The final brackets of tanka read were those composed by members of the Imperial Family present on the occasion. They were recited in reverse order of precedence, climaxed by the poems of Their Majesties.

Empress Michiko:

> *when they wave lanterns here,*
> *over there brightness*
> *flickers in answer…*
> *a day of travelling*
> *enters into night*

Emperor Akihito:

> *a pine torch*
> *blazes on its stand…*
> *the forest beyond*
> *begins to take on*
> *its autumn colouring*

The Empress's tanka was chanted twice, the Emperor's three times.

After that, the Imperial party ceremoniously withdrew. The invited guests were then escorted to a large anteroom, where we were presented with a tiny cup of sake, small plates of traditional New Year delicacies, and booklets of the Japanese text for all the tanka which had been recited. I only wished we had been permitted to have these booklets to read during the proceedings; that would have made it much easier to follow the tanka meanings, which were often obscured by the highly stylised form of chanting with which the poems were presented.

Ten minutes was allocated for the consumption of the sake and snacks, while we stood at long trestle tables. After that we were escorted to our waiting black limousines (taxis not being allowed in the palace grounds).

The entire proceedings in the Pine Tree Hall had been discreetly televised, and were shown live on TV on the NHK Cultural Channel.

Attending the *Utakai Hajime* of 2008 was a truly memorable experience for me. It was a most impressive display of Japanese cultural gravitas. Surprisingly, there was no music of any kind at the event. The national anthem was not played. The tanka were chanted by unaccompanied voice(s). There was no applause; the audience maintained total silence throughout.

And I could never have imagined the solemn visual impact of the Emperor, and some 112 other gentlemen (most of whom had shiny black hair), wearing formal morning suits with black jackets and grey trousers. The court ladies were all in pastel, Western-style, long frocks, with matching gloves and tiny hats.

Coming out into the palace grounds at noon, I blinked in the bright sunshine of a crisp January day.

In the Autumn of My Life

as I stroll through drifts of dry leaves in Canberra with the four-legged darlings, images of another park, and a border collie, float behind my eyes.

In Seattle now, my grandchildren will be scampering with Gypsy around the spring lake.

It is sadly symbolic: their blossoming so far away, and our light fading here. I try to keep up in spirit, but…

>   *reluctantly*
>   *ending our weekly call*
>   *I embrace them*
>   *with my voice, always*
>   *only with my voice*

The Love Affair Continues: Japan, May 2010

brown hawk
hovering above the paddies
undisturbed
by this train speeding
through his spring valley

Hidatakayama

wisteria
humming with drunken bees
in the mauve sunshine
I am remembering
how I loved this place

one small girl
under a big pink hat,
standing safe
within the straddled portals
of the mountain god's shrine

sounds of water,
crimson azaleas
by the canal…
oh, little yellow bird
I was happy here once

a white swan
one solitary swan
on this lake
over the long years
I have come here to dream

you can see
that my hands are old,
but do you know
how young is my heart?
new green shines in the fields

Nara

from my window
on the hotel's sixth storey
coloured lights
blurring in dark night rain…
will all be clear tomorrow

Hokkeiji Temple

rain pooled
in glass-like fragments
on lotus leaves
gleaming and shifting as
the sun returns to the pond

Issuien Gardens

along the limbs
of an old old pine
light reflected
from the water, rippling
flickering, fading

nudging aside
crimson waterlilies
a brocade carp
flashes its black and gold
through the opaque pond

Futaji Temple

to the music
of a bush warbler
yellow butterflies
waft above purple iris
at Narihira's temple

seated beneath
perfumed clouds of white
wisteria
celebrating in spring
the autumn of our lives

Daisy Chains

On closer examination, the myriad tiny daisies embroidering this lawn are not all white: some have petals tipped with pinky-mauve; others are entirely crimson.

The children are doing handstands, while their dog rolls over in summer exuberance.

Below a scarlet azalea hedge, the ground slopes down to the still water.

> *Mt Rainier*
> *a floating snow-white cone*
> *in clear blue sky*
> *beyond the sunlit bay*
> *another life beckons*

Yellow Balloons

The first time I meet the poet, I am surprised to see how tiny she is. A huge creativity married to a sprite-like physicality.

In her tanka, and in our conversations over the following ten years, she talks to me of her favourite things: feathers and plum blossoms; babies and daffodils; blue autumn air; cosmos flowers, and balloons…especially bright yellow ones.

Yūko loves everything light.

Eventually the cancer thins her to a little voice in a fragile husk.

greying, a sunset cloud
drifts beyond the horizon

Time Passes

Nagatani...
my eager mind, my fond heart
no longer seek
the way to the house
by the bamboo grove

'What do you want with my wife's work?'

'I want to translate it.'

'Can you do that?'

'Yes, I can.'

And so began my journey with a fascinating companion and no defined destination.

Of our first stage, collaborating on her 1995 tanka collection, *Time Passes*, Kawano Yuko (1946–2010) wrote this:*

lifting her eyes
which had been fixed
on my third tanka,
she says 'ever'
is better, more poetic

one by one
my words are transformed
into English
with the gentle flexing
of her pencilled letters

---

* in her book *My Tanka Diary* published in 2002, translated by Amelia Fielden

Aside from ultimately translating six of her books, I was privileged to make two television programs with Yūko, and to participate in her Tower society's tanka workshops whenever I was in Kyoto at the right time.

Outside NHK studios, Tokyo	a workshop at Kyoto University
I wanted *to say how much I* *admire her,* *but we parted there* *still talking of plum jam*	*fluttering* *her Kyoto fan* *she glances* *round the respectful room,* *sighs a sensei's* sigh*

Standing in her beloved cosmos garden as she farewelled me, eleven years after I had first journeyed to meet her, Yūko whispered, 'Only a few more years, that's all I want…'

There were to be no more years, just a few more months.

though the grove
still rustles and talks
in her tanka,
the Nagatani Shrine gods
were deaf to her prayers

soon they will bloom
white pink mauve crimson –
the poet is gone
never to return home
to her cosmos garden

---

* 'sensei' is the Japanese term for 'teacher'.

Just Sitting There

When I board the bus from the pre-dawn street my gaze stumbles on the first occupied seat.

By the window sits a bulky young woman. Pressed against her is a small white and tan dog, smiling,

I offer the back of my hand to the dog while a fellow passenger observes, 'If that's a Jack Russell, it's pretty quiet.'

'Yes,' responds the young woman. 'At the shelter she was just sitting there, like she was waiting for me.'

> *'can this be love?'*
> *the shelter terrier*
> *rides to town*
> *with her companion*
> *in a matching sweater*

The Longest Week

> *'see you soon,*
> *the end of March,' we said*
> *hugging and*
> *kissing her goodbye*
> *for the very last time*

The call comes, as such calls are wont to do, in the darkness just before dawn.

I ring around the family interstate and overseas, regardless of the early hour or time differences.

Then we dismantle the holiday house, pack the car, in bewildered haste. How? Why?

> *all the trees*
> *are still in summer-green leaf,*
> *our daughter only*
> *thirty-eight years old*
> *the morning she doesn't wake*

We drive inland for five hours, to the capital.

Homecoming is the same as always…and not at all the same.

> *she is gone…*
> *butterflies are dancing*
> *the sun still shines,*
> *but nothing will shift*
> *this boulder on my chest*

After a long week of making the arrangements no parent ever wants to make, we hold her funeral.

Outside the chapel the young ones release brightly coloured balloons into the air.

>*the red balloon*
>*seems to ride on the wind*
>*becoming a dot*
>*high on the blue sky, then*
>*disappears into a cloud*

'now that April's there'*

in Seattle 2010

>despite the grief
>that has flown with me
>across the world
>in Seattle it is
>cherry blossom season
>
>let me describe
>the magnolia tree
>in full bloom
>beneath it daffodils
>this spring you cannot see
>
>my room still fogged
>with dreams of elsewhere
>at seven
>the low thrum of traffic
>filtering through bird calls
>
>revisiting
>the unpredictable
>the slow days
>at home with young kids
>again…at sixty-nine

---

* a phrase from the poem 'Home Thoughts from Abroad' by Robert Browning (1812–1899)

in the playground
by falling peach blossoms
a child swings
higher into the sky
of her imagination

across the clouds
across a patch of blue
an eagle
soars effortlessly…
survival of the fittest

damp grey skies
scampering squirrels
white hyacinths…
with one warm small hand
in each of mine, I walk on

Forgotten Lane
a signpost by the pines…
some paths
not taken, others mapped
in happy memory

black and white dog
paddling a pewter lake,
round the shores
all the colours of April:
fond photo to take back home

Ups and Downs

My challenge for today: accomplishing some clothes' shopping for myself while entertaining my lively five-year-old grandson.

The first part is easy; a bus ride into the city always provides amusement – especially for the other passengers, as Stephen has a loud, clear voice, an interesting vocabulary and few inhibitions.

The streets are jostling, the choice of shops extensive. I eschew the boutiques with bits and bobs in easy reach, make for a multistoreyed department store.

Four escalators up to the women's fashion floor, and it's evident how this excursion will play out.

Twelve escalator trips later, I have two new shirts, one jacket, a pair of trousers, and a small boy ready for lunch at the market creperie.

> *'down again*
> *Grandma, up again' –*
> *no one else's*
> *imperative voice*
> *would I smilingly obey*

Black Butterfly

no other word
but 'dancing' could describe
the progress
through the Zen garden
of a black butterfly

So much of what I love about Japan is here, in the grounds of this old wooden temple. A hundred metres and several hundred years up the cobbled lane from a major thoroughfare, such peace.

at noon, empty
of priests and worshippers,
the temple precinct
thrums with the transience
of summer cicadas

My guide today is my dearest Japanese friend, Nariko.

There is a deep understanding, and almost half a century, in our relationship.

How fortunate I am, to sit with her now, sipping green tea under the veranda eaves as we silently contemplate that dancing butterfly…

Discovering Gabriola Island, British Columbia
July 2011

from the ferry between Anacortes and Sidney on Sea

>two seagulls
>perched on a short plank
>facing
>in opposite directions
>as they drift through the straits

Sidney on Sea

>at the harbour
>so many shades of blue
>we agree
>on scenic beauty
>though not on much else

Gabriola Island: from Sonya's terrace

>otters in the mist :
>through swaths of grey satin
>over the bay
>ripples widen, dark heads
>surfacing, disappearing

poetry composing walk near Naomi's home

> beside her man
> contemplating haiku
> in the rain
> stands a stoic terrier
> on Drumbeg beach

from the narrow roads of the interior, on Gabriola Island

> 'ocean spray' –
> all along the verges
> tall bushes
> hung with creamy bunches
> of these tiny flowers
>
> green green grass
> appliquéd with woolly brown
> alpacas…
> nothing on this island
> reminds me of home
>
> a deer steps
> from the enchanted forest
> with two fawns
> frisking close behind…
> the tremble of summer leaves

Not a Love Song, But…

red parasols
under a blizzard
of blossoms,
the Japan we know
from picture postcards

And *I* know from over half a century of intimacy with the 'country upstairs', that has included innumerable cherry blossom viewing visits, *hanami*, to parks and shrines and beauty spots all over its islands.

The precise Japanese term for cherry blossoms is *sakura*. Yet so intrinsic are cherry blossoms to the Japanese aesthetic that the generic term *hana* 'flowers', when used in poetry, is assumed to mean 'cherry blossoms'.

Now…into an Australian coastal spring, not a cherry blossom within coo-ee here…comes our eight-year-old blue-eyed blonde granddaughter from Seattle.

'I've got a surprise for you,' says Haylie, seating herself at the piano. Then she launches into the traditional Japanese folk song, 'Sakura Sakura', accompanying her playing with a sweet-voiced version of the lyrics in English.

with the charm
of her new music,
the miracle
of her existence,
she joins my worlds

Stars in My Eyes

reading, always
reading and writing
stories, poems,
while other kids played outside
or rode their bikes around

Ever since I understood what it meant, I wanted to be a journalist.

Gold stars for my 'compositions'.*

Editor of the school magazine.

A cadetship with the *Sydney Morning Herald*. I was on my way…

And then, the seduction of a scholarship to study Japanese in Canberra.

'Come back to us when you graduate' – last words of the *Herald* editor-in-chief as he waved me off to university.

But the trajectory of my life moved me further and further away, from Canberra to Tokyo to London to Malta to Morocco.

Kind Mr Leck was long gone when I finally returned to Sydney.

at seventy
so much to recollect
of what has been,
still time to ponder
what might have been

---

* In my schooldays a composition was a piece of imaginative writing.

Brief Idyll in Busselton, April 2012

Prelude: he sleeps softly
        steadfastly, through the night
        I wrestle
        with old memories
        and new intentions

Introduction: Finally, we have gathered them all – save for dear lost Kerstie, and the 2+2 living in Seattle. Our children and their partners, and our grandchildren, including the family from distant Stockholm. Here in Western Australia for a much anticipated and tightly planned reunion.

Not under one roof: a single Sandy Bay chalet cannot accommodate fourteen of us; but we're close enough to call out, 'Good morning. How did you sleep?' and 'Did you hear those possums in the night?'

10 April 2012: pale day moon
black and white wagtails
in the dunes,
and I'm swimming
a morning meditation

two brothers
drawn from afar by the death
of their sister,
standing waist-deep together
in the Indian Ocean

11 April:

    beachside sunset
    orange flames fading
    to a pink glow,
    then flights of parrots
    grey-winged by the dusk

    almost dark
    just the flutter of her skirt
    against the swing
    shows our granddaughter
    from Sweden, here at last

12 April: Paradise Regained

    to sleep
    to the cadence of the sea
    to wake
    to a symphony of birds
    and the cadence of the sea

    onto the beach
    prances a retriever –
    protesting
    seagulls rise, resettle
    to ride the gentle waves

13 April: fleeing a chaos of breakfasts, I return to the sea: yes, this is a dogs-permitted beach

                      chasing rabbits
                      chasing each other
                      little white dogs
                      darting through the dunes –
                      how I miss our two

14 April: swallows weaving
                      dipping and dancing
                      at the shore
                      how shall I, wingless,
                      express my joy

15 April: today's sea is grey
                      petulant as a child
                      deprived of fun,
                      no swimmers breast the waves
                      gulls huddle on the sand

                      tentacles
                      uncoiled, pandanus palms
                      wave left, right
                      treading water in the storm
                      I too must survive

16 April: still standing
ankle-deep in the ripples
a lone shag –
is there some decision
to be made here?

17 April: jellyfish sting
easily creamed away,
not so
this sense of paradise
soon to be lost again

18 April: kick, kick, kick –
teaching another child
to swim
independently
the waters of this life

19 April: the passage
from horizon to shore
of a speedboat
no swifter than the passing
of my seventy years

And so the visit ends, with lots of photos and hugs – but no promises.

21 April 2012

Today would have been the eighty-ninth birthday of my mother, Muriel Alice Mason.

Today is the tenth birthday of my female labradoodle Konjiki 'golden coloured one', known to many in Canberra and at Buff Point as Konni.

We note the date; but we don't feel celebratory at Konni's ageing into double figures, although she is still very healthy and absolutely full of beans.

Konni and her older half-brother, Kin, have been inseparable since we brought Konni home from her breeder's place in Condobolin when she was six and a half weeks old, a tiny auburn-haired pup with long, long legs and an assertive temperament.

Konni quickly developed a fierce passion for ball-playing, a passion not shared by her more laid-back brother.

> *sunset lake*
> *bonsai islands darkening*
> *as the air blurs*
> *we're searching in frog sounds*
> *for her purple ball*

They both love running free in the great outdoors, though.

> *a warm wind*
> *Kin and Konni swimming*
> *tumbling racing*
> *across the beach together*
> *this is life, this is joy*

May 2012: Another Autumn in Canberra

More than a year since the passing of our youngest daughter.

Though we had retired to a more temperate coastal climate, her father and I returned often, and for long periods, to support Kerstie in Canberra.

Kerstie is gone; so too her pain and problems.

There is an altered rhythm of life for us here now.

> *each day the same*
> *each day so different –*
> *two stars still*
> *in the lightening sky*
> *of our capital home*

The seasons revolve, all with their own simple pleasures.

> *May morning*
> *a stillness of white clouds*
> *in azure bright*
> *I empty my mind, fill it*
> *with chrysanthemums*

> *garden party:*
> *from beyond gold-leafed trees*
> *in Madonna-blue skies*
> *cathedral bells ring out*
> *this autumn afternoon*

> *quiet courtyard:*
> *as the sky exhales*
> *a single leaf*
> *falls onto my tanka*
> *in last year's journal*

On the Edge

bringing back
'those lazy, hazy, crazy days
of summer'
with my grandchildren
in the US of A

Unexpectedly it's sunny and warm in Seattle every day this second week of August. Both kids are still on vacation from school. The easiest and most fun way of spending time together is to walk to the lifeguarded 'beach' at the nearby lake, where they can swim and play to their hearts' content.

Stephen is only seven, not tall for his age.

Excelling at backstroke, he is also a competent diver. And totally fearless. He swims out through the deep water to a pontoon with two diving boards. For starters, he executes a perfect running dive from the low board. Next, he does a forward somersault off the same board. The gaggle of teenagers on the pontoon starts to take notice.

Nonchalantly, Stephen climbs the ladder to the high board.

At the very edge – what a showman – he peers downwards, opens his arms in a gesture of 'will I, won't I', then goes for it.

on the high board
a diminutive figure
against the blue
he pauses…jumps,
slices into the lake

Egged on by the teenagers, Stephen follows up with a forward somersault…from the HIGH diving board.

An understatement, to say that I am on edge while watching this display!

> *back on shore*
> *he snuggles onto my towel,*
> *munching cookies…*
> *I can relax and bask*
> *in the pleasures of love*
>
> *lazing now*
> *I lie on my side*
> *in the grass*
> *beneath summer's blue skies,*
> *lush-leafed birch branches*

The Piano Lesson, 13 August 2012

       beneath the painted gaze
       of Wolfgang Amadeus
       a girl child
       fingers his sonatina,
       piano, pianissimo

       next, small brother
       obeying their teacher
       bounces the keys
       to produce a tune
       both light and lively

       finally
       a sibling duet is played
       with assurance…
       two fair heads held high,
       four tanned legs dangling

And So To Asilomar

There are several stages of pleasure I experience before going to Asilomar, on Monterey Bay in California, for the four-day Haiku Pacific Rim and Yuki Teikei poetry festival of 2012.

First of all, I share the last month of their summer vacation with my two young grandchildren at home in Seattle.

> *wind chimes plus*
> *the flags of two countries*
> *on this porch*
> *a temporary peace,*
> *a place for simple love*

> *black cherries,*
> *plump, juicy and sweet*
> *reminiscence*
> *of family feasts*
> *in Sydney's Decembers*

At Karkeek park

> *the 'bubble man'*
> *sends his frail creations*
> *into the blue*
> *a seagull flies higher,*
> *over the chirping children*

An old friend comes to visit

> *after a year*
> *in opposite hemispheres*
> *we carry on*
> *with the same conversation*
> *accompanied by sushi*

Then, only days later, tragedy strikes her

> *summer gardens*
> *grow giant sunflowers*
> *heavy-headed*
> *my friend deals with the death*
> *of her only son*

The next week I take the children across Puget Sound by ferry to picnic with another poet friend, who lives on Bainbridge Island.

> *'Grandma,*
> *do you remember*
> *those two seagulls*
> *hovering over our ferry*
> *all the way, the last time?'*

The last time was almost two years ago, and I marvel again at what young children recollect.

During my final week with the family, we continue the tradition of spending a few days in Captain John's Cottage by the ocean in Oregon. The weather is blessedly fine and warm, so most of our waking hours are spent at Indian Beach.

> *wetsuit donned*
> *my body floats the waves,*
> *spirit soaring*
> *with clouds of brown pelicans*
> *across the bright horizon*

On the last day the young ones hire reclining bikes, and race around at low tide on the sands by Haystack Rock. Walking home we are enchanted by the sight of five wild otters at play:

> *from the bridge*
> *over the stream at dusk,*
> *my family*
> *watches a family*
> *of otters frolicking*

Back in Seattle, a final visit to Green Lake playground before I fly off to San Francisco and later return to Australia.

> *warm sunshine*
> *on September second*
> *in the park*
> *kids comparing teachers*
> *for the coming school year*
>
> *two crows*
> *shiny black, sitting*
> *atop*
> *a giant pine tree –*
> *what will he say next*
>
> *still majestic,*
> *a dying fir thrusts*
> *rusty-brown*
> *towards silver aircraft*
> *skimming the clear blue sky*

And so to Asilomar: first a flight to San Francisco, where I meet up with a posse of out-of-town poets. Next day, travelling together on a minibus we stop off at Point Lobos, Wolf Point, to meet the local Monterey poets and indulge in a lavish picnic lunch.

Last time I was here, in September 2008, I was told the story of how the early explorers heard the sounds of seals on the shore, and mistook them for wolves. So I wrote this:

> *from below*
> *a fog-narrowed cliff path*
> *the barking*
> *of harbour seals*
> *not wolves, never wolves*

Today there is no fog when I stroll around this state park. I see small, tough wildflowers, pink ones and yellow ones, in rocky crevasses and

> *unexpectedly*
> *the twitching of deers' tails*
> *in a thicket*
> *filled with gruff echoes*
> *from the seal colony*

Odd, later, to find myself accommodated at the conference centre village in the same 'craft movement' suite I had shared with Arthur almost four years earlier, where:

> *lying in bed*
> *separated at length*
> *we discussed*
> *the cathedral ceiling*
> *of our shingled cabin*

On the first day of the poetry festival, I dutifully, and interestedly, attend all of the morning and early post luncheon sessions. On the 'gingko walk' afterwards, I write no haiku, but wander alone by Monterey Bay.

> *in the dunes*
> *looking for wild life*
> *I find*
> *driftwood, a dead mouse*
> *and tiny white daisies*

The evening meal in the communal dining hall is early, and the days are still long. So after we have eaten, some of us go down to the beach again and linger, admiring aloud the miraculous sky as the sun sinks right into the waves.

> *seagulls flap*
> *through the brilliant sunset*
> *of a west coast –*
> *switching allegiance*
> *I reset my watch*

Another fine day follows:

> *bright-sky morning:*
> *a blue jay flies low, lands*
> *again*
> *I affirm that is*
> *my most loved colour*

On our final morning, the bay is wild, a darker blue than ever, surging with great white-foamed breakers.

> *louder today*
> *that teal autumn ocean*
> *beyond*
> *the rhythmic rise and fall*
> *of reciting voices*

Goodbye, goodbye, to Asilomar, to America…

Wisteria

I fly from California to Western Australia, where my dear husband has been staying with his sister while I was away, and arrive in Perth the day before a significant birthday. For the first of several celebrations, we three A. Fieldens – Arthur, Ann and Amelia – go to lunch at a charming restaurant in a suburb near Ann's home.

Outside the front door is a small Japanese-style rock garden.

This restaurant is situated alongside a martial arts school; display cabinets full of the school's memorabilia line the shared entrance.

We are seated on a sunlit patio under shade-cloth sails.

While the menu which we are handed lists only modern fusion dishes – not a sushi in sight – we are facing a lovely Japanese 'stroll garden'. Alas without a camera.

after coffee
a saunter round the grounds
carefully
stepping the mossy stones
over the koi pond

mauve wisteria
draping over an arbour
forms the frame
of our mental snapshots –
he is eighty today

so many years
of Japanese gardens
here and there
white narcissus in bloom
summer warmth scented with spring

My Golden Boy

Our cream and gold, curly-haired miniature labradoodle was born on 1 October 2000 – in the middle of the Sydney Olympic Games period.

I called him Kintaro, after the boy hero of Japanese folklore. This name means 'golden lad', and it seemed appropriate, also, given the newspapers' daily headlines at the time, of gold, gold, gold!

Of course I love his sister, Konni, too – and I have loved many other pets in the past – but Kin is my once-in-a-lifetime, oh so special, pooch.

Now he is twelve years old, and more precious than ever.

> *my little dog*
> *the velvety feel of his skin*
> *on my arms*
> *the soft puffing of his breath…*
> *more than a decade, this love*
>
> *your heart beats*
> *across my seated thighs*
> *you sleep secure,*
> *but a dog's life is short*
> *what will become of us*

The Element of Water

Poetry and water – poetry the active agent of my three days in Ishikawa prefecture, water the ever-present passive, lying in great silent expanses on my consciousness.

This adventure begins in an aircraft descending over Tokyo Bay, and it ends in another flying south over the ocean to Sydney.

Changing planes at Narita to a domestic service, I am transported over the Japan Alps – still snowless in early autumn – to Komatsu beside the Japan Sea. I am surprised by the stillness of this stretch of grey-blue below, as the plane circles low before landing. So often I have seen the Japan Sea, on TV or on movie screens, raging and heaving in winter blizzards.

The provincial roads are smooth and fast, and the poet's car soon gets us to the small city of Kaga. Then over the Benkei Bridge, which commemorates a historic thirteenth-century battle fought here, to the venue for our first performance, the Snow and Ice Museum.

The three-dimensional snow-crystal-shaped architecture of this edifice is more stunning in reality than on the pamphlets I have seen. And the setting: the museum stands, set back a little from the water, on the shore of a vast natural lagoon.

Between the upper floor of the museum and the lagoon, a 'fog garden' of volcanic rocks slopes down to a small glass-walled café which appears to float on the water.

Bordering the museum is a park with slender canals leading to the lagoon, and long avenues of *sakura*, cherry blossom trees still lush-leafed in their summer green. This is the prime beauty spot for *hanami*, flower-viewing picnics in spring, I am told.

A stroll across the park brings us to our accommodation for the two-night stay in Kaga. This is the multistoreyed maze called the Kaga Hot Spring Inn. Its concave structure curves around the shoreline of the lagoon. There is not room even for a footpath between the inn and a narrow strip of sand.

Sitting in the enclosed balcony of my fourth-floor tatami-matted suite I seem to be floating above a field of waterlily pads.

Around three o'clock, a small pleasure boat, old Japanese style, with curly-sided roof and hanging lanterns, comes into view gliding across from the far-side of the lagoon to a short jetty at the end of the cherry blossom park. The railings of the jetty wobble bright silver reflections onto the water. A little later three high school kids turn up on their bicycles, which they abandon on the grass while they play at skimming stones through the lily pads and pretending to push one another into the lagoon.

Off centre towards the west, a fountain I hadn't noticed in the lagoon suddenly spouts up and out in the shape of a giant arum lily: water from water into water.

White Mountain in the far distance is blurred dark blue background to the sunset, as just one bright pink cloud drops into the lagoon.

> *near twilight*
> *four ducks sailing abreast*
> *through lily pads*
> *over the grey lagoon –*
> *where should I send my thoughts*

At night the fountain is illuminated in fluorescent green. With the image of bright green spraying on black, I close my eyes.

The next evening is our concert of *shinobue* flute music, and trilingual poetry in Japanese, English and Latvian, held in the elegant performance space on the top level of the Snow and Ice Museum.

For the concert finale, the doors are opened to the balcony so that the audience can watch and listen to the husband and wife duo as they play their flutes on the opposite side of the fog garden. There they stand, dim outlines in kimono, just above and beyond the clouds of steam rising from the garden, swirling in spectral patterns, drifting out onto the dark lagoon.

Sunday begins more prosaically with a two-hour drive along a freeway to the city of Tsuruga, where, in the cavernous conference room of a Western-style hotel, Mari Konno and I present papers on 'The Internationalisation of Tanka' to a large provincial forum of studious poets.

Our route now to Fukui detours to a pit stop café and viewpoint high above the Japan Sea coast village of Suizu. After the twenty-five minute speech I've just made in Japanese, I appreciate the soothing effects of a 'coffee float' ice cream on my throat. From the back balcony of the café I see how clusters of mountains really do slope right into the sea. Randa, the guest performer from Latvia, enlightens me that there are no mountains in her country.

Mari, who went to Latvia to launch her tanka collection, *Snow-crystal * Star-shaped* – the book which I translated and which has brought us all together at this point in time, during the Poetry Days in Riga festival of 2010 – contributes that what the Latvians call 'waterfalls' are only trickles, a couple of metres high, in their rivers.

When we arrive to check in at the Annex Hotel Fukui, I find it is built on the edge of a stone-walled moat, all that remains of an ancient castle. My window opens outwards, above the moat; I'm surprised to see a number of small tortoises in the water, as well as the ubiquitous carp.

There are many, many more carp, brocaded in gold and silver, black, blue and orange, with amazing patterns, swimming in the pond of the old *daimyo* mansion to which we walk for a rehearsal of that evening's event.

It seems to me that the pond is larger than the traditional house itself.

For our concert, all the internal screen dividers between the tatami rooms are removed, to make a single long space. The performers are to stand at one end amid banks of perfumed flowers; the audience – some sixty strong – will sit and kneel on the floor beyond. We use the smaller 'moon-viewing' annex as a changing and waiting room.

> *no moon in view*
> *from this moon-viewing room*
> *only a slow*
> *circle of light-coloured carp*
> *on the darkening pond*

This early autumn night is mild and still. Most of the external wooden walls have been slid open, too, so that the pond, with its swishing, gulping carp, becomes the backdrop to the performances.

Magic: there is no overhead electric lighting, just a discreet sprinkling of *bonbori* floor lamps inside the rooms, candles and ground lights around the pond.

Across the pond's stepping stones come the flautists, their music quivering through the balmy air, drifting into the enchanted mansion.

> *autumn evening:*
> *trilling of bell crickets*
> *not silenced*
> *by the silver sounds*
> *from shinobue flutes*

> *I hear still*
> *in my Australian dreams*
> *flute music*
> *among the swirling mists*
> *across a night-dark pond*

Not in an Aviary

an unknown bird
at daybreak singing me
from blackness
into the pastel promise
of a new spring day

There is a plethora of birds where I live – both in the garden city of Canberra and in the small coastal town of Buff Point/Budgewoi, north of Sydney: from common sparrows, pigeons, pelicans, seagulls, to Eastern rosellas, sulphur-crested cockatoos, kookaburras, and pink and grey galahs, they are a constant presence and a constant delight.

So much part of my life are wild birds that they naturally, and frequently, find their way into my poetry. I remember being surprised, ten years or so ago, when my stepmother Nita reported that a friend to whom she had lent one of my tanka collections asked whether I like birds – because there were such a lot of birds in the poems!

Of course – I love birds, I observe them all the time, I write about them. But I don't really like to see them caged.

When I was a schoolgirl, the Scottish family in the flat below my grandparents in Coogee kept a bright yellow canary in a cage hung on a sunny balcony. He sang the most brilliant songs.

the golden trill
of a caged canary
shimmering
those hot afternoons
I read Great Expectations

The one time I have had caged birds in my own family was in a Tokyo apartment in the early 1970s, where they were the only pets permitted.

Even then, we used to let the two budgerigars out of their large cage at least once a day.

> *free playing*
> *in our Tokyo kitchen*
> *lovebirds*
> *one blue, one yellow*
> *and my two small girls*

For the most part, the birds in my poetry are wild birds, all kinds of wild birds, I watch wherever I go.

In Seattle

> *a bald eagle*
> *snatching a young crow –*
> *how to justify*
> *survival of the fittest*
> *to my watching grandchild*

> *in the reeds*
> *a red-winged blackbird sings*
> *for its mate –*
> *so little response from you*
> *to my emails*

At White Fish Lake, Montana

> *teal ducks calling*
> *in this different time zone*
> *I fret*
> *over familiar woes, until*
> *a freight train takes them away*

At Asilomar, California

> *separated*
> *by a single wall,*
> *the magpie-lark*
> *summoning me outdoors*
> *is my new best friend*

On the Gold Coast of Queensland

> *sparrow, way up high*
> *chirping, bouncing along*
> *the balcony edge*
> *outside its safety railing –*
> *oh, if I had wings*

In Sydney

> *frustration:*
> *eventually the pigeon*
> *pushes that Cheezel*
> *off the station platform, then*
> *pecks at a smaller crumb*

At Mossy Point, on the South Coast

> *dyed by the dawn*
> *flamingo-pink seagulls*
> *on the sandbar*
> *a dog barks   suddenly*
> *they fly heavenwards*

> *winter's end:*
> *through the cool blue sky*
> *black swallows*
> *cavorting with abandon*
> *before an early sunset*

In Canberra

> *rosellas*
> *red and blue, flash past,*
> *two into a tree*
> *one onto a concrete pole –*
> *the 'whys' of this life*
>
> *can that be*
> *the same scarlet parrot*
> *breakfasting*
> *high in our plum tree?*
> *yesterday I was happy*
>
> *white cockatoos*
> *flying the cloudless blue –*
> *just one year*
> *after her death, I'm trying*
> *to write some joyful tanka*

At The Entrance on the Central Coast

for 'pling

> *estuary*
> *puffin on a pole –*
> *recalling*
> *your bird photographs*
> *I send you this tanka*
>
> *two pelicans*
> *side by side at low tide*
> *barely paddling,*
> *floating on the here and now*
> *our backs to the horizon*

At Buff Point

> *a white heron*
> *stands on its reflection*
> *in the mirror-lake*
> *the stillness needed*
> *for my shifting heart*
>
> *not expecting*
> *a colony of black swans*
> *at the jetty*
> *I'm contemplating the nature*
> *of this random world*

And everywhere, the magpies

> *at sunrise*
> *a sparkling chorus*
> *of magpies*
> *cancels the forebodings*
> *from my sleepless night*
>
> *lake glistening*
> *frost spiking the grass*
> *magpies calling*
> *from grey-green eucalypts:*
> *those old jogging winters*
>
> *winter hill:*
> *a magpie scavenging*
> *in the snow*
> *summer memories*
> *half-buried like first love*

Hydrangeas – for Elinor

Early in the final month of the first year of the new millennium, you came from far in the north.

Since your previous visit, we had acquired a new member of the family: a miniature labradoodle puppy, only two months old when you arrived in Canberra.

It had been a damp spring, and the big hydrangea bush in our back courtyard was dense with pink blossoms.

A very pretty sight, my husband crouching in the front of the hydrangea with little Kintaro in his arms. You took several photos of them. The smilingest one still stands on my bureau, framed in silver.

Almost twelve years have passed since that colourful moment you captured with your camera.

The hydrangea bush has not survived the drought years in between, and our frequent absences from home.

Yet happily we welcome you again, dear friend.

> *no hydrangeas*
> *and youth's bloom has left us all –*
> *yet we are here*
> *still loving life, grateful*
> *for these days together*

Home for Christmas 2012: Back to the Beginning

> *'home for Christmas':*
> *and for those without homes*
> *without families –*
> *how do they celebrate*
> *in this festive season*

Living in comfort in a peaceful country, I am lucky and I know it. My family members may be scattered but there is a lot of love amongst us all. Always I have had a home, a family and love.

My first homes were in Coogee, a beachside suburb of Sydney. And for twenty-one years, before I began worldwide roaming, I spent Christmas Day in the small Coogee flat of my maternal grandparents. Gran and Pop lived with much happiness in aptly named Arcadia Street.

Every twenty-fifth of December, number 23 Arcadia Street bulged with family and festive foods: great-grandmother, grandparents, parents, uncle, aunt, cousins, together for roast turkey, plum pudding with silver threepences in it, walnuts, black cherries, beer and soft drinks chilled on great blocks of ice in the bath.

Faces shining with the heat of a sunny, sultry Sydney day, then watching from the back window for a cooling 'southerly buster' to roar in across the sea late in the afternoon.

> *southerlies*
> *riding white horses*
> *through the bay*
> *forever in rhythm*
> *with grandmother's tales*

This year, exactly half a century since my last Christmas in Coogee, a very different scene. Rather than a modest flat near the northern end of the beach, it is a four-star hotel at the southern tip where my husband and I are spending Christmas with our daughter Kathleen and her life partner, 'pling.

As soon as I look out of the hotel bedroom window on Christmas Eve, I see the spire of St Nicholas Anglican church, a short distance up the hill. How appropriate: St Nicholas, the original Santa Claus.

Before Dad moved us to Canberra when I was ten, I went faithfully to Sunday school at St Nicks. Not a regular churchgoer for many years, I am drawn now to the Christmas morning service.

'hark the herald angels sing'

Wonderful the peace of sitting again surrounded by the stained-glass windows whose stories I hadn't forgotten.

More nostalgia and the same feeling of ease, later, when I immerse myself in the sea pool where my father taught me to swim all those decades ago.

> *fifty years…*
> *how far I have travelled*
> *to come home*
> *like a twilight seagull*
> *to Coogee's white sands*

Afterword: 'I'll be seeing you in all the old familiar places'

Although Japanese tanka collections customarily include an 'afterword' written by the poet, I had no such intention for *Mint Tea from a Copper Pot*. I planned for it to end with my tale of Christmas 2012 at Coogee.

Then, on 2 January 2013, I came home from the post office where I had just mailed the completed manuscript to my publisher, to find in my laptop inbox, the saddest of news: a dear friend in Seattle had passed away there unexpectedly on 29 December.

Jay was already in this book: in the piece 'And So To Asilomar', she is the unnamed 'old friend' who came to visit me in August and who shortly afterwards was devastated by the accidental death of her only son.

We met again in September for the poetry gathering at Asilomar, where we walked by the shore, shared mealtimes, had quiet drinks in Jay's room after the evening seminars. And of course in this tanka I wrote, there is a double-entendre with her name

> *bright-sky morning*
> *a blue jay flies low, lands*
> *again*
> *I affirm that is*
> *my most loved colour*

Our friendship was book-ended by haiku: we had found each other at the Haiku North America conference in Portland, Oregon, in the northern summer of 2009, and three years later we were participants in the Haiku Pacific Rim festival in California.

Travelling back from Monterey to San Francisco on 9 September after HPR, Jay and I sat next to each other on the minibus. On arrival outside my hotel in Japan Town, we hugged and said not 'goodbye', but 'see you next year'.

That was not to be.

In memory of Jay, my special 'buddy' – her word – I'd like to add here four of the tanka I had composed in her company during some of the Seattle outings we enjoyed over the years.

by Green Lake

> *the haziness*
> *of a Japanese myth:*
> *twin cherry trees*
> *with blossoming branches*
> *entwined   trunks apart*

> *footpaths fringed*
> *with buttercups and daisies*
> *everywhere*
> *the scent of roses –*
> *a storybook summer*

at the Kubota Gardens

> *dwarf maple*
> *all of its limbs greened*
> *with soft moss –*
> *and when the rolling stone*
> *has finally settled?*

in the Seattle Japanese Gardens

> *so trustingly*
> *the willow's trunk leans out*
> *over the pond*
> *propped by a stout pole –*
> *my love has slipped away*

Vale Jay Gelzer

Acknowledgements

The following pieces in this book have already been published, several in slightly different or abridged forms, and/or under different titles. For their assistance and appreciation, I thank the editors of the relevant publications.

Prologue: *The Tanka Journal*, 2010, No. 36, edited by Aya Yuhki

In the Twelfth Month: *Modern Haibun and Tanka Prose*, 2009, edited by Jeffrey Woodward

Night Games: *Magna Poets*, 2012, edited by Aurora Autonovic

My First and Only *Miai*, and Of Love, Marriage & *Kanji*: *Downunder Japan*, 2012, edited by Graham Bathgate

Mint Tea from a Copper Pot: *Atlas Poetica* journal, internet special 2011, edited by Bob Lucky

'Aye, there's the rub': from *Elemental Moods*, a haibun renga collaboration between Anne Benjamin, Amelia Fielden, Jan Foster, Marilyn Humbert and Keitha Keyes, edited by Jan Foster and published in *Lynx* 28:1, edited by Jane Reichhold

'Please Sir, I want some more': excerpted from my *Still Swimming* tanka collection 2005, edited by Kathleen Bleakley

After the Storm, a Rainbow Lorikeet: *Animal Encounters* anthology, 2012, edited by Catchfire Press

A Tale of Two Cakes: *Haibun Today*, 2012, edited by Claire Everett

Through the Looking Glass: *Light on Water*, 2010, my most recent book-length tanka collection, edited by Ellen Weston

The New Year's Tanka Poetry Gathering at the Imperial Court in Tokyo: *Moonset* newspaper, 2008, edited by an'ya

In the Autumn of My Life: from *Elemental Moods*, ibid.

The Love Affair Continues: *The Tanka Journal*, 2011, No. 38, edited by Aya Yuhki

Yellow Balloons: from *Elemental Moods*, ibid.

Time Passes: *Haibun Today*, 2010, edited by Jeffrey Woodward

Just Sitting There: *Light on Water*, ibid.

The Longest Week: *Haibun Today*, 2011, edited by Jeffrey Woodward

'now that April's there': *Kokako*, 2011, edited by Patricia Prime

Discovering Gabriola Island, British Columbia: *The Tanka Journal*, 2012, No. 40, edited by Aya Yuhki

Brief Idyll in Busselton: some of the tanka in this piece were published in *The Tanka Journal*, 2012, No. 41, edited by Aya Yuhki

About the Author

Born in Sydney in late 1941, translator and poet Amelia Fielden has subsequently experienced life in Japan, England, Morocco and Malta, as well as in several states of Australia.

Currently she and her husband Arthur, and two labradoodles, move between homes in Canberra and on the coast north of Sydney. Their grandchildren live in America, Sweden and Western Australia, so Amelia continues to travel. Other passions are swimming, reading, ballet – and, of course, Japan.

Amelia is committed to lifelong learning and has a penchant for universities. Spanning more than half a century, she has gained variously, degrees, diplomas and research experience (in this order), from the Australian National University, Canberra; Nagoya University and Tokyo University, Japan; the University of Adelaide; the University of Queensland, Gold Coast Campus; the University of Newcastle, NSW; The Frontier University, Ube, Japan.

Since 2002 specialising in the work of contemporary Japanese women writers, Amelia has produced eighteen volumes of Japanese poetry in translation.

In 2007 Amelia and co-translator Kozue Uzawa were awarded the Donald Keene Prize for Translation of Japanese Literature by Columbia University, New York, for their anthology *Ferris Wheel: 101 Modern and Contemporary Japanese Tanka* (Cheng & Tsui, Boston 2006).

Amelia's latest work of translation is of a book compiled by Nagata Kazuhiro after his wife, the famous Kawano Yūko, passed away in 2010. Entitled *For Instance, Sweetheart: Forty Years of Love Songs*, it is a large collection of essays and tanka written by these two poets.

The following books of Amelia's original writings have also been published.

Eucalypts and Iris Streams, English poems, with Japanese translations by Saeko Ogi, Ginninderra Press, Canberra, 2002

Fountains Play, English tanka, with Japanese translations by Saeko Ogi, Ginninderra Press, Canberra, 2002

Short Songs: A Collection of English Tanka Poems, Ginninderra Press, Canberra, 2003

Still Swimming: Tanka Poems, Singles and Sets, Ginninderra Press, Canberra, 2005

Baubles, Bangles & Beads: Threaded Tanka, Ginninderra Press, Canberra, 2007

Light on Water: Tanka Poems, Ginninderra Press, Adelaide, 2010

In Two Minds, Amelia Fielden and Kathy Kituai, Modern English Tanka Press, Maryland USA, 2008

Yesterday, Today and Tomorrow, Amelia Fielden and Kathy Kituai, Interactive Press, Brisbane, 2011

Weaver Birds, Saeko Ogi and Amelia Fielden (bilingual Japanese/English), Ginninderra Press, Adelaide, 2010

Words Flower – From One to Another: a responsive tanka collection (bilingual English/Japanese), Amelia Fielden and Saeko Ogi, Interactive Press, Brisbane, 2011

Amelia has also had her work published in many international journals and anthologies. In addition, she has edited two anthologies of themed tanka poetry:

Food for Thought: an anthology of new tanka on a theme by 45 Australian poets, Amelia Fielden, editor and contributor, Ginninderra Press, Adelaide, 2011

The Melody Lingers On: an anthology of tanka on musical themes written by 55 Australian poets, Amelia Fielden, editor and contributor, Ginninderra Press, Adelaide, 2012

www.ingramcontent.com/pod-product-compliance
Lightning Source LLC
Chambersburg PA
CBHW071009080526
44587CB00015B/2395